BATS

OF CARLSBAD CAVERNS
NATIONAL PARK

by

Kenneth N. Geluso

J. Scott Altenbach

Ronal C. Kerbo

D1668722

© 1987 Carlsbad Caverns
Natural History Association
3225 National Parks Highway
Carlsbad, New Mexico 88220

ISBN 0-916907-01-5

Flying Mammals

About 900 species of bats exist in the world today. The only mammals more diverse are rodents with approximately 1700 species. Bats live nearly everywhere on the earth except Antarctica, the coldest parts of the Arctic, and some oceanic islands. Thirty-nine species inhabit the continental United States; only one species occurs in Hawaii and four in Alaska. Fifteen of the 25 species found in New Mexico live in Carlsbad Caverns National Park. In addition, fossil remains of one extinct species have been discovered within the park's boundaries. The bats at Carlsbad Caverns represent only two of the 18 families of bats — the Free-tailed Bats and Common Bats. Appendix 1 lists the common and scientific names of bats found at the park.

Although there are mammals called flying squirrels and flying lemurs, these animals do not fly; they can only glide. Bats are the only mammals that actually fly. Bat wings are thin membranes of skin attached along the sides of the body and hind legs and braced by elongated bones of the forearm, palm of the hand, and fingers. The short, clawed thumbs and clawed toes remain free of the membrane. Despite their thinness, these elastic membranes resist tears and punctures. To the touch, they feel somewhat rubbery. Powerful chest and arm muscles provide power for wing movement during flight. The smallest bats have wingspans of only five and a half inches, but the largest bats reach five and a half feet across. At Carlsbad Caverns, wingspans range from nine inches in the western pipistrelle to 17 inches in the big free-tailed bat.

Many bats, including all those at Carlsbad Caverns, also possess a tail membrane — a double layer of thin skin stretched between their hind legs and tail. In the Free-tailed Bats, as the name implies, most of the tail projects beyond the outer edge of the tail membrane when the bats are at rest. In flight this membrane can be slid backwards towards the tip of the tail. In the Common Bats, tails are enclosed by the membrane for most or all of their length when bats are at rest or in flight. Although these tail membranes may not be necessary for flight, they certainly must help increase aerial maneuverability. Tail membranes also are used as scoops to assist insect-eating bats in catching prey in midair, as pouches to receive baby bats during delivery, and as blankets to help foliage-roosting bats conserve body heat.

Orientation by Sound and Sight

Faces of many bats look peculiar because of their oddly shaped and often enlarged ears; leaflike projections and other elaborate structures on or around their noses; and wrinkles, lumps, and bumps on their lips. Studies indicate that many of these structures assist bats in echolocation, the means by which bats perceive their surroundings in darkness. Ultrasonic sounds are emitted through a bat's mouth or nose. These sounds echo from nearby objects and are picked up by its ears. Facial structures help bats direct outgoing sound waves and receive echoes. This method of orientation allows bats to avoid striking objects in their path and to locate, identify, and capture tiny moving prey in total darkness. The term sonar also describes this form of orientation. Most ultrasonic sounds produced by bats cannot be heard by humans; however, bats also produce audible sounds that are used primarily for communicative purposes between and among bats. Future research may show that bats also use ultrasonic sounds to communicate with each other.

Previous page:
Evening flight of Mexican free-tailed bats as seen from inside the mouth of Carlsbad Cavern.

In Mexican free-tailed bats, as the name implies, most of the tail projects beyond the trailing edge of the tail membrane.

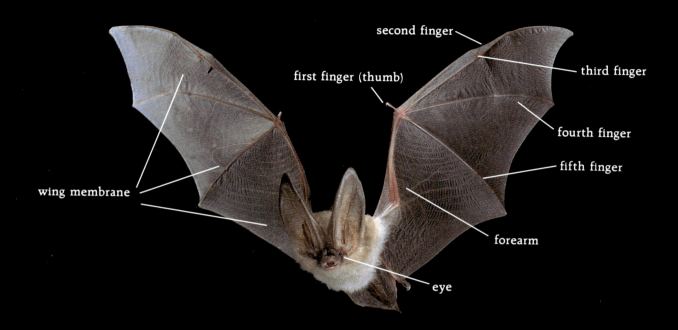

second finger

third finger

first finger (thumb)

fourth finger

fifth finger

wing membrane

forearm

eye

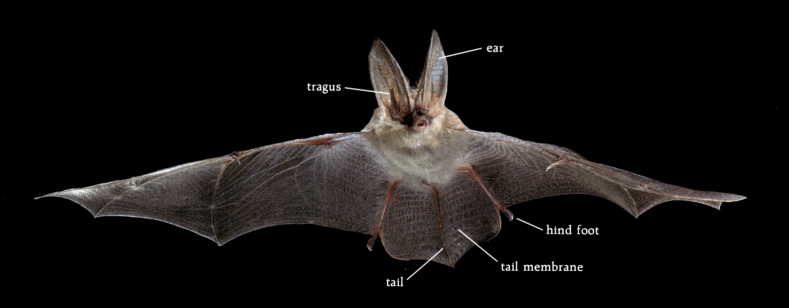

ear

tragus

hind foot

tail membrane

tail

The unique appearance of bats is largely a result of their specializations for flight, as illustrated by Townsend's big-eared bats.

All bats have eyes and can see but not all bats can echolocate. The few species (about 160) that cannot acoustically orient rely on their relatively large eyes to guide them and to locate food. Although the echolocating species, including all those at Carlsbad Caverns, depend heavily on sound and usually have small eyes, vision still plays an important role in their lives. For one thing, the production of sound waves is energetically expensive; by using vision whenever possible, bats conserve energy.

Sense of smell is also important to bats. Many species have characteristic body odors due to secretions of glands located on various parts of their body. Among Carlsbad bats, Mexican free-tailed and pallid bats have the most readily noticeable odors to man. Odors are used to mark territories and aid mothers in locating babies. Bats also find food like flowers and ripe fruits by smell. Olfaction may even help bats locate caves.

High-frequency sounds emitted through the mouth of this California myotis echo from nearby objects and are picked up by its ears; this allows the bat to orient in darkness.

Insect-eating Bats

Most bats in the United States and all those found at Carlsbad Caverns eat insects. They feed primarily on moths and beetles although mosquitos, flies, grasshoppers, cockroaches, termites, flying ants, and many other insects also are consumed. While flying, bats use their tail membranes and wings to scoop insects out of the air. The extent to which they capture flying insects directly by mouth remains to be determined. Some bats fly among branches of trees and seize prey off foliage with their mouths. Some species also forage on the ground, catching

flightless insects and other ground-dwelling animals. For example, pallid bats prey upon such flightless forms as Jerusalem crickets, darkling ground beetles, sun spiders, scorpions, centipedes, and small lizards.

Insect-eating bats have a tremendous ecological impact by controlling the size of insect populations. At one time it was estimated that about 8.7 million Mexican free-tailed bats resided at Carlsbad Cavern, the main bat cave in

Faces of many bats such as Townsend's big-eared bats (left) and Mexican free-tailed bats (above) look peculiar because of their oddly shaped and enlarged ears, lumps above their snouts, and wrinkles on their lips. Many of these structures assist bats in echolocation.

the park. During one summer's evening, such a population could consume about 100,000 pounds of insects from the surrounding area. This estimate is based on the fact that bats consume about a third of their body weight in insects each night, with pregnant and nursing females eating as much as half their weight.

In the United States and other temperate regions, insect-eating bats use two strategies to cope with low supplies of insects during colder months. One strategy is to leave the region and migrate to warmer locales where insects are still available. One of the best examples of bat migration is the millions of Mexican free-tailed bats that temporarily leave the United States each autumn and head for Mexico. Some travel more than 800 miles to reach their winter destinations.

The other strategy is to remain in the region and hibernate. In preparation for hibernation, bats accumulate excess amounts of body fat. Then they seek shelters where temperatures will be cool enough to allow them to conserve energy. Caves, mines, and cellars often provide suitable hibernating sites. During hibernation, bats lower their body temperatures — some to just a few degrees above freezing. This allows them to use their fat reserves slowly until spring arrives and their food supply reemerges. Bats hibernating in the Carlsbad area and other southern locations may become active during warm winter evenings to drink and to feed on active insects. Both migrators and hibernators inhabit Carlsbad Caverns National Park, and some species employ both strategies to deal with winter food shortages.

In addition to hibernation in winter, many bats also can conserve energy on a daily basis during warmer months. By selecting shelters away from the heat, bats can drop their body temperatures to surrounding air temperatures during part of each day. Reduced body temperatures plus accompanying drops in metabolic and breathing rates not only conserve energy but also reduce the loss of water through the respiratory tract. How much free-tailed bats take advantage of this daily torpor is unclear at this time, but other bats at Carlsbad Caverns are known to use it or are highly suspected of using it.

Pallid bats are unique among bats at the park because they feed on flightless insects and other ground-dwellers such as this large centipede.

Bats as Pollinators and Seed Dispersers

Three species of bats that live in parts of the Southwest, but not in Carlsbad Caverns, feed on nectar and pollen of certain plants. Hovering for short periods in front of blossoms, these bats thrust their long tongues deep into flowers of such plants as agave and cactus to gather nectar. Although some pollen is obtained directly from flowers during this process, most of it is swallowed as bats groom themselves after foraging. Nectar is rich in sugars and high in water content, while pollen provides needed proteins. Some of these bats supplement this diet with insects, small amounts of fruit, and flower petals. The majority of flower-visiting bats live in tropical and near-tropical regions; those inhabiting the United States apparently respond to the scarcity of blossoming flowers in winter by migrating south. Because these bats are continually dusted with pollen as they travel from blossom to blossom, they are important plant pollinators. Similar to some plants that have evolved specialized flowers to attract birds and insects, plants that depend on bats for pollination have done the same. Bat-pollinated flowers, for example, open at dusk and at night, produce large amounts of nectar, and usually have strong musky odors to attract bats. For many plants such as saguaro cactus, balsa trees, and some agaves (including those used for making tequila), bats are the primary agents of pollination.

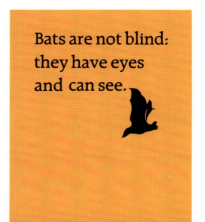

Bats are not blind: they have eyes and can see.

Fruit-eating bats live in the tropics where there is a continuous and rich supply of fruits throughout the year. Some prefer soft, ripe fruits while others select extremely hard ones. Some supplement their fruit diet by eating insects, leaves, and flower products such as nectar and pollen. Fruit-eating bats are extremely important in dispersing seeds of tropical plants. Bats chew fruits with their flattened teeth, swallowing the juice and pulp while spitting out seeds and fibrous materials. Because bats often carry fruits in their mouths to distant tree roosts before eating, seeds are widely scattered from the parent tree. Small seeds that are swallowed pass through the bat's digestive system unharmed and eventually are deposited wherever the bat defecates. Although these bats primarily feed on wild fruits, some consume economically important ones such as bananas, mangos, avocados, papayas, and figs. In these cases bats are considered agricultural pests. Recent field studies in mango plantations, however, indicate that bats are eating only those fruits that are too ripe for harvesting. Laboratory observations show that this probably is the case for the other fruits as well.

Bats are mammals: they have hair, and mothers nourish their young with milk.

Blood Drinkers and Meat Eaters

Vampire bats are the only mammals that feed entirely on blood. Only three species are known and all inhabit the Western Hemisphere, ranging from northern Mexico to central Argentina and Chile. Adults weigh approximately one and a half ounces and have wingspans of about 16 inches. One species feeds primarily on the blood of mammals, including humans, another prefers the blood of birds, and the third consumes both mammalian and avian blood. Vampires make small incisions with their bladelike incisor teeth and lap up blood with their tongue. An anticoagulant in the bats' saliva prevents blood from clotting while they are feeding. Adult vampires probably consume about one fluid ounce of blood each night.

Vampires have given bats a bad reputation concerning rabies. Because of their feeding habits and because rabies virus is contained in saliva, infected vampires spread the disease whenever they feed. Infection rates of bats in areas where vampires are absent are low or nonexistent. Recent surveys in California, for example, indicate that 1 in every 1,000 bats that appear normal is rabid — an occurrence lower than in wild carnivores such as skunks and foxes. Furthermore, bats are not "healthy carriers" of rabies as mistakenly suggested by early studies; like other mammals they either become paralyzed and die after infection or they survive exposure without spreading the disease. Occasionally, downed Mexican free-tailed bats from the park have been tested for rabies and found to be positive for the virus. The best advice to the public concerning bats and rabies is never to handle bats found on the ground, even if they appear to be dead.

Meat-eating bats inhabit regions in both the Old World (including India, Southeast Asia, and Australia) and New World (including Mexico and Central and South America). As a group their prey consists of fish, frogs, lizards, birds and mammals, including other bats. All supplement their diet with insects and some occasionally eat plant material. The fish-eaters also consume small aquatic crustaceans. All animal-eating bats have powerful bites with long canine teeth used for piercing and holding prey. Bats specialized for capturing fish have long hind legs with feet possessing long, sharp, curved claws. These bats fly low over the surface of water while hunting for food. After detecting fish movements at the water's surface by echolocation, bats drop their large hind feet into the water and impale their prey. Fish are then hauled out of the water and are eaten in flight or at some convenient perch.

Much less is known about the hunting behavior of the other carnivorous bats; however, scientists have observed these meat-eaters diving down and plucking singing frogs from sides of ponds, entering houses to pick lizards off walls, and chasing and capturing other bats in flight.

Reproduction and Life Expectancy

In most mammals including Mexican free-tailed bats, eggs are fertilized by sperm soon after copulation. However, a majority of hibernating bats do not follow this basic pattern. For these species most matings occur in the fall prior to hibernation, but fertilization does not take place then because eggs have not yet been released into the female's reproductive tract. Instead, sperm are stored in the female's uterus and they remain there alive throughout winter dormancy. Eggs are shed and fertilized soon after females emerge from hibernation. With delayed fertilization, there is no waiting for males to produce sperm in early spring. This pattern allows maximum time for young to mature, to learn to fly, and to store fat for the upcoming winter. In addition, it permits adults to attain breeding condition and to copulate during late summer and fall when their energy supply (insects) is plentiful. Delayed fertilization is known to occur in nine species inhabiting Carlsbad Caverns — the big brown bat, cave myotis, fringed myotis, long-legged myotis, California myotis, pallid bat, red bat, silver-haired bat, and Townsend's big-eared bat. Little is known about the breeding habits of the remaining bats at Carlsbad Caverns.

An infant Mexican free-tailed bat clings tightly to its mother while nursing.

A few mammals are known to lay eggs, but bats give birth like most other mammals. Litter sizes in bats range from one to five young per pregnancy, but most species give birth to one young at a time. Twinning is common in four species residing at Carlsbad Caverns — the western pipistrelle, pallid bat, silver-haired bat, and hoary bat. The red bat usually has more than two young per litter, sometimes as many as five. The remaining species at the park normally deliver only a single young. All bats at the park produce only one litter annually, but a number of tropical species have multiple litters each year.

A Mexican free-tailed bat becomes a meal for a Trans-Pecos rat snake. Although many types of animals will eat bats if the occasion arises, very few animals regularly prey upon bats.

Bats have noticeably low reproductive rates, as stated above, especially when compared to similar-sized rodents which typically have many young per litter and several litters each year. Bats partly compensate for this by living much longer than rodents. A conservative estimate for the average life span of a bat after surviving its first year is about 10 years. Records of 15-year-old and older individuals living under natural conditions are not uncommon. One bat has been known to survive at least 30 years in the wild. Small rodents, on the other hand, usually live no longer than a few years; nevertheless, because of their much higher reproductive rates, they still end up producing more young per mother than bats.

Being eaten by other animals is a major reason for short life expectancies of ground-dwelling rodents. Because bats typically roost in inaccessible places and forage in flight, they are relatively free of predators. Although many types of animals will capture and eat bats if the occasion arises, few predators

consistently feed upon bats. For many years at Carlsbad Cavern, great horned owls perched on a ledge just above the large natural entrance. Each evening during the outflight, owls would fly among the bats and catch them in midair with their claws. They consumed the bats after returning to the ledge. Other regular predators of bats include the bat hawk of Africa, a few tropical bats, and some snakes. In parts of Africa and Asia bats are regularly eaten by people.

Like all mammals, mother bats produce milk in mammary glands to nourish young during their initial period of growth. Females have only one pair of functional glands. A baby is usually born tail-end first and begins to nurse soon after birth, latching securely onto one of its mother's nipples with tiny, hooked teeth and onto her body with claws of its feet and thumbs. Eventually the teeth are shed and replaced with permanent ones. In some species, young are born with hair on their bodies; others initially enter the world naked.

Roosts: Where Bats Hang Out

Bats spend the majority of their lives roosting. Because they forage at night and at twilight, most roosting is done during daylight hours. Even during the night, however, bats may spend much time resting and digesting between feeding bouts at some convenient roosting site. Night perches also include places for fruit-bats to eat their fruits, meat-eaters to await their prey, and others to call for mates. During the cold winter months, hibernating bats may roost up to three months.

When not roosting in man-made shelters, big brown bats roost in hollow trees, rock crevices, and caves. Humans frequently encounter this species because it often roosts in buildings.

Bats commonly roost in caves and their man-made equivalents including mines, cellars, and other tunnel-like structures. Rock and tree crevices, tree cavities, foliage, and a wide array of locations inside and outside buildings also are favorite haunts. In fact, almost anyplace a bat can hang up or squeeze into could be, and probably has been, used by a bat at one time or another. Roosts provide bats protection from predators and, depending on their location, also shield them from unfavorable weather. While under this protection, bats can rest, sleep, hibernate, eat, digest, hunt, groom, communicate, mate, give birth, and raise young.

Most bats roost by hanging upside down by the claws on their toes. Some cave-dwellers also use the claws of their thumbs to hang onto ceilings. Those that squeeze into rock crevices, behind loose bark, or other tight places may be completely supported by the substrate itself. A few species of bats that roost in vegetation have small suction cups on their wrists and feet to help them hold onto smooth surfaces like leaves and the jointed stems of bamboo. Bats do not build nests, but some do modify their roost environment. For example, a few species cut the main veins of leaves with their teeth, causing the leaves to bend over and to form an overhanging shelter. Using their teeth and claws, two New Zealand species excavate tunnels into rotting logs where they subsequently roost.

A small cluster of cave myotis hangs from the ceiling of a gypsum cave. Clustering helps to conserve heat and to minimize evaporation of water through the skin.

Most species of bats inhabiting Carlsbad Caverns seek shelter in rock crevices or caves, but some such as the red bat and hoary bat prefer to hang in the foliage of trees. Although there are some man-made structures in the park and a wide variety of vegetation, it is the caves and rock fissures, crevices, cracks, and crannies that provide bats with abundant roosting opportunities.

A red bat hangs among the leaves of a peach tree. Roosting red bats sometimes resemble dead leaves and certain kinds of fruits.

Bats' Habitat

Eastern escarpment of the Guadalupe Mountains. This long ridge is the remains of a fossil reef that formed along an inland sea millions of years ago. The flat landscape represents what was once an ancient seabed.

Most of Carlsbad Caverns National Park is in the Guadalupe Mountains of southeastern New Mexico. These mountains form part of the northern boundary of the Chihuahuan Desert, most of which is in Mexico. The park encompasses 73 square miles of land and is located southwest of the city of Carlsbad in Eddy County. The visitor center is a 27 mile drive from the city.

Geological History

The limestone and dolomite that make up the park's caves, cliffs, valleys, and rock outcroppings are the remains of an ancient reef that formed along the edge of an inland sea more than 250 million years ago. The rocks of the reef are actually skeletal remains of small lime-secreting organisms plus calcium carbonate crystals derived directly from seawater. After the reef formed, waterways supplying the inland sea closed and the sea slowly began to dry up. As the water evaporated, the entire region leveled off as sediments composed of gypsum and salts were deposited on the sea floor and filled in its huge basin. Then a few million years ago, mountain-building forces pushed up the entire area. Eventually, the softer sediments of the sea basin eroded, leaving the harder limestone and dolomite as a mountain range, the Guadalupes. Standing in front of the park visitor center and looking to the southwest, one can see a long, curved ridge called the Guadalupe Escarpment that clearly marks the edge of the old reef. Also in view are hundreds of square

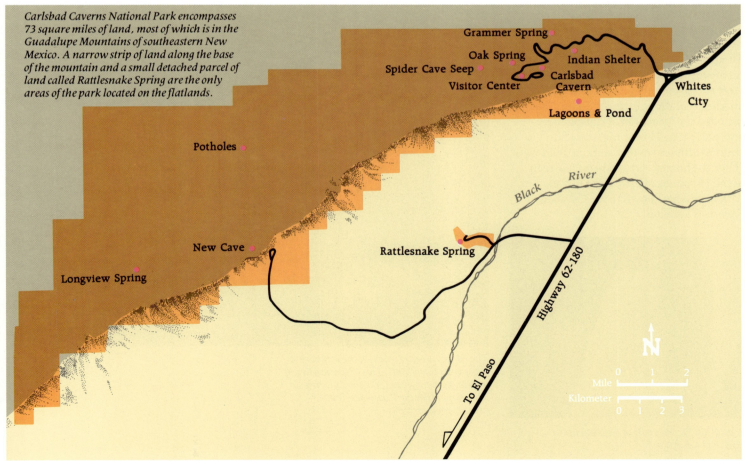

Carlsbad Caverns National Park encompasses 73 square miles of land, most of which is in the Guadalupe Mountains of southeastern New Mexico. A narrow strip of land along the base of the mountain and a small detached parcel of land called Rattlesnake Spring are the only areas of the park located on the flatlands.

Grammer Spring

Oak Spring

Indian Shelter

Spider Cave Seep

Carlsbad Cavern

Visitor Center

Whites City

Lagoons & Pond

Potholes

Black River

New Cave

Rattlesnake Spring

Longview Spring

Highway 62-180

To El Paso

N

Mile   0   1   2

Kilometer   0   1   2   3

miles of relatively flat landscape which represents what was once the ancient seabed.

Although most of the area in the park lies on the reef, a small detached unit called Rattlesnake Spring is located on deposits of the flat seabed. This 80-acre site is approximately five miles south-southwest of the visitor center. A natural spring on this property supplies water to the visitor center and other buildings in the cavern area. Not surprisingly, Rattlesnake Spring represents the lowest surface elevation within the park's boundaries (3,650 feet above sea level). The only other part of the flat seabed in the park is a narrow strip of land that runs along the base of the reef. In contrast to these lowlands, the elevation of the visitor center is 4,406 feet, but other places in the park exceed 6,400 feet in elevation.

Carlsbad Caverns National Park is known primarily for its numerous caves, the most famous of which is Carlsbad Cavern. More than 70 other caves also have been discovered in the park. Cave-building began millions of years ago when slightly acidic underground water seeped through cracks in the massive rock formations and gradually dissolved the rock. This action eventually produced large and complex caves throughout the Guadalupe Mountains, including Carlsbad Cavern. As the reef was uplifted above the water table and the rooms slowly filled with air, the decorative processes began. This included the formation of stalagmites and stalactites. These processes still occur to a limited extent and continue to shape the homes of many bats. Fourteen of the 15 species of bats found in the park have been known to use Carlsbad Cavern as a shelter.

A dead bat becomes part of a stalagmite in Carlsbad Cavern.

Climate

The climate of the Carlsbad region is characterized by low amounts of rainfall, mild winters, and hot summers. Average precipitation for the cavern area is about 15 inches per year with over 75 percent falling during the warmer months, May to October. Winter snow occasionally falls, but it never remains on the ground long. The area also is subjected to periodic droughts. Average high temperatures for July and January are 83° and 55°F, respectively. During the last several decades, the record high in July was 106°F and the record low in January was −4°F.

The rugged, rocky terrain of the reef hosts a great variety of plants. This green vegetation growing among gray rocks gives the surface landscape of the park its characteristic gray-green coloration.

Vegetation

The rugged, rocky terrain of the reef hosts a great variety of plants. This green vegetation which grows among the gray rocks, boulders, and ledges gives the surface landscape of the park its characteristic gray-green coloration.

Some of the best known and most easily recognized plants in the park include cacti, agaves, and yuccas. For example, prickly pears with their broad, flat stems are among the most conspicuous and abundant cacti. Other common cacti include several species of cholla and a number of smaller cacti popularly called hedgehog, pincushion, button, and barrel cacti. Lechuguilla, present in great abundance, is a small narrow-leaved agave with sharply pointed and slightly curled leaves. Its much larger relative, the New Mexico agave, is limited to higher elevations of the reef. Yuccas are represented by several species in the park with soap-tree and Torrey yuccas being the largest. Sotol also is common on the reef and is often mistaken for yucca, but unlike yucca, its leaf margins bear hooked spines.

The reef also contains a fair variety of shrubs and trees. The more common shrubs include ocotillo, catclaw acacia, algeritas, cat's-claw mimosa, mariola, mescal bean, and sumac. The trees are small, and most occur in relatively cool and sheltered canyon bottoms or along dry washes that infrequently contain water. The largest trees usually are found near springs and seeps. Gray oaks, desert willows, Texas walnuts, Texas madrones, and junipers are some of the more common species. Junipers and oaks also occur on exposed slopes and high ridges of the rugged canyons. Common grasses that grow in scattered clumps between the shrubs, succulents, and trees of this rocky terrain include gramas, tridens, and muhlies.

Traditionally park visitors were told that vegetation on the reef is representative of the Chihuahuan Desert. This is true to a certain degree; however, the lower portion of the reef is better considered a transitional area where desert species such as lechuguilla are mixed with plants commonly found at higher elevations. This unique mixture of plants may be easily observed in areas surrounding the visitor center and cavern entrance and along the nature trails. Plant communities at higher elevations of the reef (usually above 5,000 feet) normally do not support desert species. Sotols, New Mexico agaves, junipers, oaks, and a number of grasses are some of the more common plants at these higher elevations.

Vegetation found in the Chihuahuan Desert also is present in the open flats of the ancient seabed. Here the most common plants are creosote bushes. These medium-sized shrubs grow somewhat evenly spaced over the desert

floor. In many areas creosote bush shares the seabed with tarbush and acacias. In sandy and disturbed areas, mesquite also may be common. Common grasses of this habitat include tobosa, three-awn, tridens, and gramas. In addition to grasses and desert shrubs, agricultural fields are located where the Black River cuts through this flatland, and large cottonwoods and other deciduous trees grow intermittently along its banks. Besides the strip of land that lies along the base of the reef, the only part of this desert flatland in the park is located at Rattlesnake Spring. This portion of the park also contains some large deciduous trees in the picnic area and near man-made structures that include a ranger station, water storage pond, and an adobe pumphouse. Bats are known to use both the trees and buildings at Rattlesnake Spring as daytime retreats.

The only other structures available as roosts are located on the reef. The cavern area includes the visitor center, employee residences, and maintenance buildings. Also there is a cabin on both Yucca Ridge and Guadalupe Ridge.

Caves, crevices, cracks, and crannies in the ancient reef provide many places for bats to "hang out."

The Park's Water Holes

Most insect-eating bats probably drink every night during warm desert evenings; however, pallid bats, western pipistrelles, and Mexican free-tailed bats may be able to survive extended periods without drinking. By excreting highly concentrated urine, these species can conserve water derived from their food to a much greater extent than other New Mexican bats. Bats drink by flying low over water and scooping up small amounts with their lower jaw. Although surface water is scarce at the park, water is available to the park's wildlife on a year-round basis from several springs and seeps. Two water holes, the ones at Rattlesnake Spring and Longview Spring, are heavily used by bats.

A water storage pond at Rattlesnake Spring provides a large open area for drinking, and at least 11 of the 15 species of bats at the park have been captured over or near this pool of water. The rock-lined pond is 115 feet by 135 feet and, in some spots, about five feet deep. The pond was constructed in 1941 and covers what was once an exposed spring. Just outside Rattlesnake Spring, bats also can drink from the nearby Black River and several man-made stock tanks.

At 5,750 feet, Longview Spring is the highest permanent source of water in the park. It is located along the southern rim of West Slaughter Canyon, overlooking miles of rugged canyon country. The long narrow pool, about 40 feet by 8 feet, lies on a ledge away from background cliffs and vegetation and affords bats unobstructed flight paths over the water. Seven of the 15 species of bats at Carlsbad are known to use this water hole.

Prickly pear cactus.

Claret cup cactus.

Other permanent water holes in the canyons that are visited by bats include Oak Spring (4,221 feet), Grammer Spring (4,232 feet), and Spider Cave Seep (4,254 feet). These watering holes are located in Walnut Canyon. They have relatively small surface areas of water, and fewer species of bats have been caught over them.

Natural rock basins that collect and hold water for a time after infrequent rains provide additional watering places for bats and other animals. At least two series of basins at the park are used by bats. One is located at 3,950 feet in Walnut Canyon. Here, two adjacent basins 30 feet in diameter lie along the base of steep cliff walls near the Indian Shelter Exhibit. The other basins — called the Potholes — run along a dry wash at an elevation of 4,646 feet in Slaughter Canyon.

At an elevation of 3,720 feet, four sewage lagoons are located on the flats along the base of the reef. Each waste disposal tank is 365 feet by 135 feet. Although bats have been observed over these lagoons, it is not known whether they are actually drinking its contents or just feeding on insects attracted to the area. Bats have not been caught over the lagoons, but three species have been captured at an earthen pond located next to the lagoons. This man-made pond contains fresh water and is 100 feet by 54 feet.

In addition to these water holes, bats can drink from pools of water found inside some caves. While roosting they also can lick water from cave walls or formations. This method of drinking is an energetically inexpensive way for hibernating bats to replenish water supplies during periodic winter arousals.

Grammer Spring in Walnut Canyon. At least two species of bats use this water hole — pallid bats and California myotis.

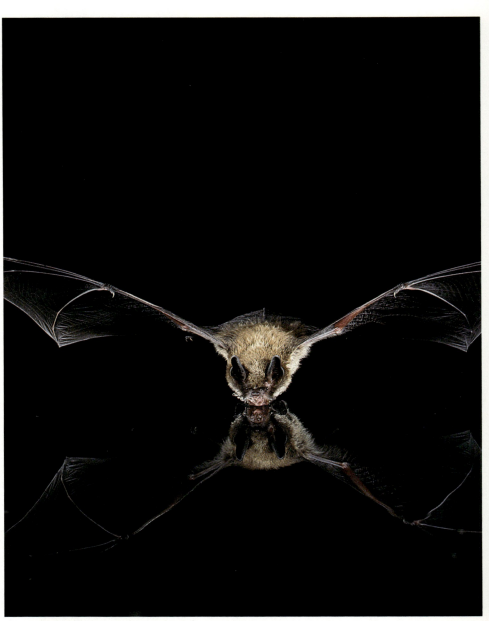

Bats drink by flying low over water and scooping up small amounts with their lower jaw. Here a long-legged myotis, mirrored in the water of a small pond, demonstrates the technique.

Much information on the biology of bats has been gathered because scientists are able to catch bats as they drink and feed over water holes. Bats are captured by stretching nets across their watering places. Multitiered nets are made of fine, pliable materials with meshes measuring about one inch square. Bats that fail to detect nets by echolocation or sight, or that detect them too late, may become entangled until removed. While holding the bats, investigators can identify them, determine their sex, age, reproductive condition, and note other information before releasing them unharmed.

A big brown bat is caught in a mist net stretched across one of the park's water holes. A biologist will record valuable information about the bat before releasing it unharmed.

Telling Bats Apart

Most bats in Carlsbad Caverns National Park can be recognized easily by observing one or two distinguishing traits. For example, four species can be identified instantly by their striking fur coloration. These include, as their common names imply, the red bat, hoary bat, pallid bat, and silver-haired bat. The remaining bats are solid shades of either brown or gray. Only two bats at the park have proportionately long ears — Townsend's big-eared bats and pallid bats. Knowing the relative body size of bats in terms of wingspan and forearm length also is helpful. These measurements are given in Appendix 2 for the bats at Carlsbad Caverns National Park.

Using these characteristics and others, we have devised a key to show how biologists identify the 15 species of bats inhabiting the park. In addition, we have included the small-footed myotis in the key. This species, which is very similar in size and appearance to the California myotis, has not yet been taken in the park, but its presence is strongly suspected. To use the key, read statements 1a and 1b. Then select the statement which refers to the unknown specimen and go to the next number indicated. Follow the sequence of numbers until the common name of the bat is reached. Many of the distinguishing traits of these bats are shown in photographs throughout this booklet.

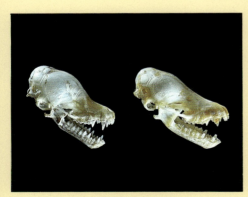

*To positively identify California myotis (**Myotis californicus**) from small-footed myotis (**Myotis leibii**), characteristics of the skull must be examined. Skulls of California myotis (left), when viewed from the side, have steeply sloping foreheads. In contrast, skulls of small-footed myotis (right) have gently sloping foreheads. The worn teeth of the small-footed myotis indicate that it is several years old.*

Key to the Bats of Carlsbad Caverns

1a. Tail projects conspicuously beyond the outer edge of the tail membrane for at least 16 mm (0.63 inches) . . . . go to **2**

1b. Tail not extending beyond outer edge of tail membrane or at most by only 5 mm (0.20 inches) . . . . go to **4**

2a. Forearm length more than 53 mm (2.1 inches) . . . . **Big Free-tailed Bat**

2b. Forearm length less than 53 mm (2.1 inches) **3**

3a. Base of ears joined across forehead . . . . **Pocketed Free-tailed Bat**

3b. Base of ears unattached across forehead . . . . **Mexican Free-tailed Bat**

4a. Ears 25 mm (1.0 inch) or more in length; ears large in proportion to head **5**

4b. Ears less than 25 mm (1.0 inch) in length; ears of normal size **6**

5a. Fur coloration brown; forearm length less than 47 mm (1.9 inches); two conspicuous lumps on top of snout . . . . **Townsend's Big-eared Bat**

5b. Fur coloration pale yellow to cream; forearm length more than 47 mm (1.9 inches); no conspicuous lumps on snout . . . . **Pallid Bat**

6a. Upper surface of tail membrane completely furred to tip of tail **7**

6b. Posterior half or entire upper surface of tail membrane naked when viewed with the naked eye **8**

7a. Forearm length more than 47 mm (1.9 inches); outer rim of ears conspicuously edged in black; fur coloration dark brown with white, grayish, or silvery-tipped hairs . . . . . . **Hoary Bat**

7b. Forearm length less than 47 mm (1.9 inches); ear margins not edged in black; fur coloration orange-red or rusty-red with some bats also having white-tipped hairs . . . . **Red Bat**

8a. Fur coloration black or blackish-brown with many hairs having white or silvery tips, especially on the animal's back . . . . **Silver-haired Bat**

8b. Fur coloration brown and without white or silvery-tipped hairs **9**

9a. Forearm length more than 36 mm (1.4 inches) **10**

9b. Forearm length less than 36 mm (1.4 inches) **13**

10a. Fringe of hair along posterior edge of tail membrane easily visible with the naked eye . . . . **Fringed Myotis**

10b. Edge of tail membrane without conspicuous fringe of hair **11**

11a. Wingspan greater than 315 mm (12.4 inches); forearm length usually greater than 45 mm (1.8 inches) . . . . **Big Brown Bat**

11b. Wingspan less than 315 mm (12.4 inches); forearm length usually less than 45 mm (1.8 inches) **12**

12a. Forearm length less than 42 mm (1.7 inches); ears blackish . . . . **Long-legged Myotis**

12b. Forearm length usually 42 mm (1.7 inches) or greater; ears light brown in color . . **Cave Myotis**

13a. Fleshy projection within ear (known as the tragus) 6 mm (0.24 inches) or more in length; tragus tapers to a narrowly rounded tip **14**

13b. Tragus 5 mm (0.20 inches) or less in length; tragus remains the same width for its entire length and ends in a broadly rounded tip . . . . **Western Pipistrelle**

14a. Foot 8 mm (0.31 inches) or more in length including the longest toe plus claw . . . . **Yuma Myotis**

14b. Foot less than 8 mm (0.31 inches) in length including the longest toe plus claw . . . . **California Myotis & Small-footed Myotis***

The Bats

Mexican Free-tailed Bat

Mexican free-tailed bats are highly colonial and most populations are migratory. Each spring millions of individuals migrate north from wintering areas in Mexico and congregate in relatively few maternity roosts throughout the southwestern United States. One such maternity roost is located at Carlsbad Caverns National Park. At these roosts, females bear and raise their single young. These young, born in early summer, reach adult proportions and begin to fly by late July. In autumn both young and adults return to Mexico.

Mexican free-tailed bats weigh less than one half an ounce and have wingspans from 11.3 to 12.3 inches. Their short, dense fur is either dark gray or dark brown. Designed for rapid and enduring flight, wings of freetails are long, narrow, and gently tapered toward their tips. This wing shape allows them to reach high speeds and to remain in flight much of the night without having to land and rest. These capabilities are essential during migration but also enable bats to scatter widely and travel long distances to and from their feeding grounds each night.

The narrowness of their wings requires freetails to maintain considerable speed to stay airborne and, as a result, freetails cannot maneuver as well in flight as can some broader-winged bats. Freetails, therefore, typically forage for insects in open areas and drink from rivers and uncluttered water holes. In the park, freetails frequently drink from Rattlesnake Spring, the rock basins near the Indian Shelter Exhibit, and the earthen pond by the lagoons. Occasionally they are netted over water holes with small surface areas such as Oak Spring.

Because of their small wing surface, freetails have difficulty taking off from the ground; however, most freetails that we tested were able to become airborne from the ground after taking a few leaps into the air. With wings folded, freetails are able to scurry about with considerable agility on the ground or on walls and ceilings of caves. Very often they crawl backwards, and the exceptionally long hairs on their toes must help them feel their way in the dark.

Mexican free-tailed bats have a very distinctive body odor that is somewhat difficult to describe in words; it is a musky smell but sometimes there is also a "sweetness" to it. This odor can be detected from the amphitheater during most evenings as bats leave the cavern through the main entrance; the more bats present, the stronger the smell.

The Maternity Roost

Visitors' journeys through Carlsbad Cavern begin by walking down switchbacks which lead through a large natural opening in a limestone ridge.

Bat Cave. The present-day nursery colony of Mexican free-tailed bats roosts on the domed ceiling at the end of this long tunnel. Guano shafts were blasted through the roof of Bat Cave in 1903 and 1906 to facilitate removal of guano. The National Park Service plugged both shafts in 1981 in order to restore Bat Cave to its natural condition. The distance from the forty-foot ladder to the present-day roost site is 600 feet.

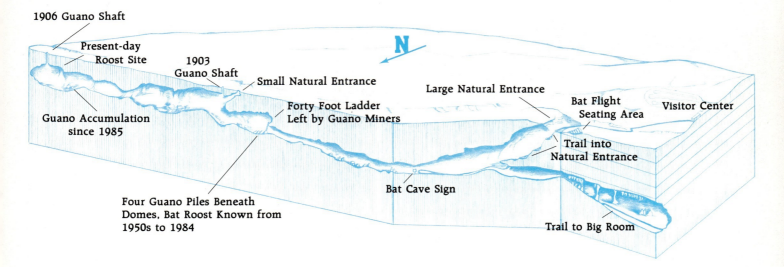

1906 Guano Shaft

Present-day Roost Site

1903 Guano Shaft

Small Natural Entrance

Forty Foot Ladder Left by Guano Miners

Large Natural Entrance

Bat Flight Seating Area

Visitor Center

Guano Accumulation since 1985

Trail into Natural Entrance

Bat Cave Sign

Four Guano Piles Beneath Domes, Bat Roost Known from 1950s to 1984

Trail to Big Room

N

The long, narrow wings of Mexican free-tailed bats are important for their rapid and efficient flight. These capabilities are essential during migration and enable bats to feed for hours on the wing.

A small number of Mexican free-tailed bats fly below a cave ceiling that is thickly covered with roosting adults and patches of hairless, pink young.

Just before making the last hairpin turn down into the main corridor and scenic rooms, visitors peer into a dark tunnel known as Bat Cave. This is the only section of the cavern known to house freetails. The present-day nursery colony roosts on the ceiling at the end of Bat Cave. Here bats hang upside down in contact with each other, covering the ceiling in single-layered clusters with up to 300 individuals per square foot.

As they constantly jockey for position on the ceiling, the bats squeak and chatter. In addition some are always flying, and the sound of their wing tips hitting and swishing through the air also contributes to the sounds below the roost. Shining a light on the colony, even for just an instant, always elicits an immediate and sharp increase in the noise level.

Because of the continuous shower of feces and urine from 100 feet overhead, standing below the maternity roost is a unique experience. The fecal pellets have a very mild odor and are composed primarily of the outercasings of insect bodies. Although these cigar-shaped pellets average only a quarter of an inch

in length, this manure can accumulate into sizable piles after decades of defecation. The smell of ammonia below the roost is derived from droplets of urine that continually soak the decomposing feces. These accumulations of excrement are called guano. Because of the large size of the cavern and its continuous air flow, the ammonia fumes are easily tolerated by man. Researchers working below the roost, however, wear masks to prevent inhalation of fecal dust and urine droplets. High protein and ammonia content make guano an excellent fertilizer, and in the early 1900s more than 100,000 tons was mined from this roost. Today guano piles are no more than four and a half feet deep.

Bats or Birds

The mild, yet distinctive, odor that is readily noticeable as one enters the mouth of Carlsbad Cavern is derived from excrement of cave swallows and bats. At night the cave swallows roost in mud nests constructed in the twilight area, the region just inside the cave entrance where daylight penetrates. These insect-eating birds spend much time circling above the main entrance

during daylight hours, and at dusk are often mistaken for bats. When bats appear, the swallows quickly settle into their nests for the night.

Evening Outflight and Morning Reentry

Each evening before dusk, bats become restless and begin to drop from the ceiling in groups. As the area beneath the roost becomes more congested, the milling bats progressively move toward the twilight area of the large natural entrance. Once they decide to depart, bats gradually gain altitude within the mouth of the cave by flying in a spiral pattern until reaching the upper lip of the entrance. Here they generally exit in a continuous and steady stream which, viewed from a distance, resembles a column of smoke.

Bats play a very important role in controlling insect populations.

Mexican free-tailed bats leave the maternity roost each evening to drink and to hunt for insects. Freetails and other insect-eating bats play an important role in controlling the size of insect populations.

On some occasions outflights are split, either with one major pause dividing the flight or with many smaller ones making the flight appear more like puffs of smoke. Occasionally, some individuals exit through a small natural entrance to the cave. Freetails leave the maternity roost each evening to drink and to hunt for insects. Small moths are their primary targets, but Mexican free-tailed bats also consume beetles, ants, leafhoppers, true bugs, antlions, flies, and dragonflies. Much foraging probably is done along the agriculturally developed Pecos River Valley and its tributaries located east of the cavern. Visitors may observe these evening outflights from a stone amphitheater in front of the large natural entrance.

Although rarely watched, the high-speed dives that freetails perform as they reenter the cavern during early morning hours also are exciting to observe. Bats approach the large natural entrance from high above and then plunge into the mouth of the cave. Dives are erratic rather than in a straight path because the bats' partly folded wings are continually adjusted to help control the direction and speed of entry. During dives you can hear a buzzing noise as wing membranes flutter from air forced over them. It is during these dives that freetails reach their highest flight speeds.

A bat flight program at Carlsbad Caverns National Park. From a large stone amphitheater, visitors await the evening outflight of hundreds of thousands of bats from the cavern.

Freetails usually emerge from the cavern in a single, continuous column but eventually break into smaller groups as they begin to disperse over the countryside.

The Life Cycle

Mexican free-tailed bats give birth to one young per year. At Carlsbad Cavern, about 90 percent of these births occur in a two-week period during late June and early July. Babies are born rump-first; they are naked and weigh nearly a quarter of their mother's body weight. While giving birth, females cling to the ceiling with both feet or with thumbs and feet. Scientists have observed mothers using their teeth to tug at emerging babies and their claws to break "water-sacs." Mothers also clean their newborn babies and some eat the placenta. Babies begin to nurse shortly after birth, latching onto one of their mother's nipples with small hooked teeth and grabbing tightly onto her fur with claws of their thumbs and feet. Most births occur around mid-afternoon. By dusk, mothers prepare for the outflight and deposit their young with other baby freetails, forming large masses of pink bodies on the cave ceiling. Freetails normally do not carry young during their own foraging flights. During the many years we have netted freetails as they left the maternity roost, we have captured only one mother with an infant still attached. Freetails, however, have been known to move young from one area to another if disturbed.

It was believed that upon returning to the nursery roost, mother freetails rarely located or even attempted to find their own offspring among the millions; instead they fed the first young that attached to their nipples. However, current studies show that mothers almost always nurse their own young.

Upon her return, a mother lands within a yard of her offspring and finds her baby by its odor and distinct calls. Other young constantly try to steal milk during this search and some unrelated bats may manage to drink for a few seconds before being brushed away. Babies are fed twice a day, once when mothers return from their own foraging bouts and again during the afternoon. When resting, mothers typically roost apart from babies.

Baby freetails grow rapidly in the maternity roost. Young reach adult proportions and begin to fly in late July, about five weeks after birth. At this time they join adults in evening outflights and begin to eat solid food. About 25 percent of flying young have milk in their stomachs, indicating that weaning is gradual. If young fall before being able to fly, they plunge 100 feet to the soft guano below. Many roll down the sides of the guano piles and frequently bump into each other, immediately clinging together and forming small clumps of baby bats. Mexican free-tailed bats do not retrieve their fallen young as do some other species of bats. Perhaps the poor lift qualities of their wings plus the fact that their guano piles are usually infested with predatory insects make it too dangerous, or often too late, to retrieve youngsters.

Tightly packed and clinging to a cave ceiling, young Mexican free-tailed bats await the return of their mothers.

Lying on guano and speckled with white mites, death is a certainty for fallen baby freetails. The milk-filled stomach of the baby near the center illustrates that both well-fed and sick bats may fall.

Guano piles at most freetail roosts are inhabited by the carnivorous dermestid beetle. When young bats or sick adults fall onto these piles, they are killed within minutes and reduced to a skeleton in an hour or two. Although the guano at Carlsbad Cavern contains a number of insects, it does not harbor dermestid beetles. Thus, fallen young are left relatively untouched and some survive five days or more on the guano before dying. Cave crickets, darkling beetles, and ground beetles living on guano at Carlsbad seldom bother young but will eat some from time to time. In addition to insects, tiny mites which fall from the roost as the bats groom and scratch themselves also land on the

guano. Mites feed on blood or flesh of bats and sometimes completely cover certain fallen individuals. During some years raccoons and ringtails discover this convenient source of food and subsequently visit the guano at regular intervals searching for grounded bats.

Typically, less than 10 percent of the babies fall from the roost and die. Some young may fall due to sickness or starvation; however, with thousands of babies pushing, nudging, squirming, and crawling over each other on a limestone ceiling, it is not surprising that some may accidentally lose their grip. One time we found a string of five babies attached to one another that had just fallen from the roost. Most likely nothing was wrong with four of the five bats except that they were clinging to a baby that slipped, and perhaps that baby slipped because four others were hanging on. In other words, a majority of fallen young appear healthy and more than 60 percent of these contain milk in their stomachs. If rescued they probably would survive.

With the onset of cold weather in autumn, surviving young and adult freetails begin their southward journey to Mexico. Frequently nonresident freetails from more northerly latitudes use Carlsbad Cavern as a stopover before continuing south. As a result, autumn outflights can be quite spectacular — not only because of the extra individuals but because flights often start around mid-afternoon. Small groups of freetails may stay in the cavern during some winters, but it is not known whether these are resident bats or ones that already had migrated from higher latitudes. The cavern's air temperature is 56°F during the winter months, and the extent to which these freetails lower their body temperature to conserve energy during this time is unknown. They may feed on insects during warm winter nights to replenish their fat supplies.

Evidently most matings occur in early spring while freetails are at their Mexican wintering grounds, but some breeding may take place during northern migration and even after arrival at the maternity roost. In Mexican free-tailed bats, sperm and eggs unite soon after copulation and embryos develop without interruption until birth.

The period of pregnancy has not been determined for freetails residing at Carlsbad Cavern, but based on colonies in Texas, it is about 90 days. Most females become sexually active during their first year of life, giving birth during their second summer.

Although bats tend to return to the same roost or at least the same area each year, many individuals do not. Many, or perhaps most, males may not even migrate north in spring but remain in Mexico. Some that migrate form relatively small groups consisting predominantly of males that roost away from large maternity colonies. Such groups have been located roosting under railroad bridges near the Pecos River, about 25 miles east of the cavern. Other migrants live in maternity roosts. At Carlsbad Cavern, adult males always are present in evening outflights but exactly where they roost in Bat Cave is unknown. Dead adult males, however, are regularly found on guano piles below the maternity roost.

Mexican free-tailed bats are found most commonly in desert and grassland habitats in New Mexico, although some individuals (mostly males) have been captured at higher elevations. These freetails are primarily cave dwellers but also roost in mines, under bridges, and in buildings. Carlsbad Cavern is the only cave at the park known to be occupied by freetails. In the United States, nursery colonies of Mexican free-tailed bats that migrate also are found in Texas, Oklahoma, Arizona, Colorado, and other parts of New Mexico. In contrast, Mexican free-tailed bats of the West Coast prefer to roost in buildings rather than caves and apparently are nonmigratory.

Population Size: Past, Present, and Future

Over the past several decades, a number of scientists have estimated the size of summer colonies of Mexican free-tailed bats in the United States. In the late 1950s and early 1960s, for example, about 100 million freetails were living in 13 colonies in Texas, nearly 7 million in 5 caves in Oklahoma, and at least 25 million at Eagle Creek Cave, Arizona.

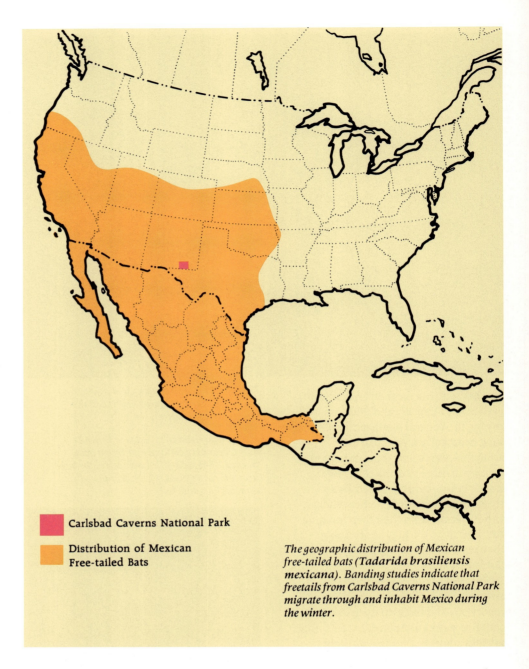

Carlsbad Caverns National Park

Distribution of Mexican Free-tailed Bats

The geographic distribution of Mexican free-tailed bats (Tadarida brasiliensis mexicana). Banding studies indicate that freetails from Carlsbad Caverns National Park migrate through and inhabit Mexico during the winter.

At Carlsbad Cavern the resident summer colony has been estimated as high as 8.7 million in 1936 and as low as 218,000 in 1973. The 1936 estimate was determined by direct observation while the 1973 estimate used photographic methods. Even if the 1936 estimate was off by millions, it is evident that there has been a major decline in population size since the late 1930s. It is not known whether the decline was gradual or abrupt. During the last decade, resident colonies at Carlsbad have fluctuated around the half million mark, with lows of a quarter million and highs of one million.

Chemical pesticides were suspected as a possible cause in this decline, and in 1973 the National Park Service began to study this possibility. Results of these studies point to the agricultural uses of DDT to kill insect pests as the probable culprit.

As baby bats mature in the maternity roost, there is a continuous buildup of pesticides in their bodies until they begin to fly; at this time most individuals contain maximum lifetime concentrations of DDT (plus its breakdown products DDE and DDD) and other chemicals. Milk is the major route for pesticide transfer to babies, but small amounts also are obtained through the placenta while they are still in the womb. Mothers accumulate most chemical residues by eating contaminated insects. Young are protected from any toxic effects during this period because they have plenty of baby fat for pesticide storage. However, as body fat is used during migration, pesticides are released into the bat's bloodstream and may reach the brain in lethal amounts. Experiments have demonstrated that pesticide levels in some flying young from Carlsbad Cavern during the 1970s were high enough to cause symptoms of poisoning if most of the stored fat was used on their first migratory flight to Mexico.

Although use of DDT has been banned in the United States since December 1972, DDT may remain in soils for decades and continue to be passed along foodchains. The cotton industry in the United States was the major user of DDT through 1972, accounting for more than 80 percent of domestic use. Cotton is grown in the Pecos River Valley where it is believed that mother bats forage. Before arriving at Carlsbad Cavern, pregnant females migrate through and inhabit agricultural areas of Mexico. At least until 1980 Mexico was one of the world's major users of DDT. However, there has been a steady decline in the use of DDT in Mexico over the last decade. At this time it is not known what portion of pesticide residues in young bats originates from the Carlsbad area and what portion is derived from Mexico. We also do not know what DDT levels existed in the bats before the ban. Studies conducted in the early 1980s show a significant drop in pesticide levels in flying young from Carlsbad Cavern when compared to the 1970s.

Guano mining operations in the early 1900s initially may have lowered the population of freetails. Suitable nursery space was reduced after a guano shaft was blasted through the roof of the main roosting site. Mexican free-tailed bats usually select spacious ceilings of large caves to form their maternity colonies. By using body heat accumulated from their huge numbers, they are able to raise temperatures of entire caves or large rooms within caves. Smaller colonies of freetails which produce less body heat can take advantage of small domed ceilings to trap warmed air.

Because baby freetails have poor control of their body temperature, high roost temperatures assure rapid growth of young and their readiness for fall migration.

Based on guano mining records of the early 1900s, freetails occupied the large domed ceiling at the end of Bat Cave plus other huge expanses of ceiling. The climate of the dome was altered after a guano shaft was drilled in 1906. Although bats most likely continued to occupy the dome for some time, the shaft probably acted as a chimney flue, letting valuable body heat escape. This would be serious in Bat Cave because it is an unusually cool chamber for a freetail roost. Eventually the large dome was not used by bats as a nursery roost for many years. It is not known exactly when this dome was abandoned and whether some bats permanently left the cavern because of the guano shaft or just moved to other areas within Bat Cave. It is known, however, that 30 years after construction of the shaft millions of freetails were still reported living at Carlsbad Cavern.

From at least the 1950s until 1984, the relatively small populations of freetails residing at Carlsbad Cavern formed nursery colonies in only four comparatively small domes located about 600 feet from the large dome. During November and December of 1981, the National Park Service plugged the guano shaft in the large dome in hopes of making it a suitable nursery site for future generations of freetails. Freetails continued to use the smaller domes to raise their young throughout the 1982-84 reproductive seasons, but in the summers of 1985 and 1986 the entire nursery colony began using a small portion of the large dome, plus a crevice in the ceiling adjacent to the dome.

History: Discovery and Guano Mining

The discovery of Carlsbad Cavern is shrouded in myths of the past. There is evidence that Indians were present in and around the large natural entrance more than 3,000 years ago. Pictographs still can be seen on the walls of the natural entrance and chips of flint and grinding tools have been found scattered near the entrance. Also, a large midden ring or cooking pit is adjacent to the modern amphitheater.

Headframes were constructed over mine shafts to allow sacked guano to be hoisted vertically out of Bat Cave.

When the first European settler in the area actually saw or entered the cave is open to debate. A local rancher named Rolth Sublett claimed to have been lowered into the entrance of the cavern by his father in the late 1800s when Rolth was only 12 years old. Another cowboy from the area named Jim White also claimed to have entered the cave around the turn of the century. No matter who was there first, a common thread runs through their tales of discovery: they were led to investigate the cave area because of "what appeared to be a large cloud of smoke or a cyclone" which turned out to be millions of Mexican free-tailed bats leaving the cavern.

As people began to explore the cave and talk about the huge amounts of guano in Bat Cave, a man by the name of Abijah Long became interested in the guano from an economic point of view. Long knew that there was a market in California for the guano to be used as a fertilizer in the fruit orchards. The market value of guano at that time was about 90 dollars a ton.

In June of 1903, Long filed a claim on 40 acres of land around the entrance of the cave and began mining operations. At the beginning, 50-pound sacks of guano were hauled out of the large natural entrance with the use of an aerial cable system. But later in the same year, a shaft was blasted through the roof of

the cavern near the small natural entrance in Bat Cave, allowing bagged guano to be lifted straight up through the shaft. For the same purpose, another shaft was drilled through the large domed ceiling at the back of Bat Cave in 1906. Once out of the cave, the sacks of guano were loaded onto wagons and transported to freight yards in the city of Carlsbad; travel time for these mule-pulled wagon trains was two days.

Because of the presence of bats during the summer, mining was restricted to September through March. Mining continued day and night, and according to one report two men could fill and tie 400 fifty-pound sacks in eight hours. By 1923 some 100,000 tons of guano had been removed from the cave.

Between 1903 and 1923 six different companies had attempted to make a profit mining guano from Carlsbad Cavern. However, prices kept declining through the years and none of the companies had a very wide profit margin. When Carlsbad Caverns National Monument was established in 1923, mining activities were halted in Bat Cave. The monument became a national park in 1930, but mining of guano still was allowed in other caves in the park, including New Cave. All mining was stopped in the park after 1957. No one managed to make an acceptable profit from guano mining; however, thanks to the freetails, attention was focused on one of the premier caves in the world. By 1985, over 26 million people from all over the world had visited the park.

Other Free-tailed Bats

Two other species of freetails inhabit Carlsbad Caverns National Park besides the Mexican free-tailed bat; both are much less common. Only one pocketed free-tailed bat and two big free-tailed bats have been collected at the park. One of each was caught as they flew through the large natural entrance of Carlsbad Cavern. The second big free-tailed bat was discovered roosting in the adobe pumphouse next to Rattlesnake Spring. The big free-tailed bats were both females (one adult and one immature) while the pocketed free-tailed bat was a nursing mother.

Bat guano is still a valuable source of organic fertilizer in many parts of the world. 🦇

Over 100,000 tons of guano was mined from Carlsbad Cavern in the early 1900s. (Above) Guano miners at work. (Below) A man is standing next to a pile of guano at the end of Bat Cave.

Unlike the huge colonies of Mexican free-tailed bats that roost in caves, pocketed and big free-tailed bats form small colonies and prefer to roost in crevices of cliffs and other rock formations. Their colonies typically contain less than 150 animals. Both species are desert inhabitants, but in New Mexico, big free-tailed bats also live in montane habitats. There are no winter records for either of these freetails in New Mexico, and the extent to which these bats migrate or perhap hibernate is unknown.

Fossil remains of an extinct freetail were discovered at New Cave in 1954. Much of the guano deposited in this cave was removed before 1957, when mining operations were halted. Bat researcher Denny G. Constantine examined skulls and long bones that he found scattered in the remaining guano and recognized that these animals were distinct from freetails presently living at the park. Subsequently a new species, Constantine's free-tailed bat, was named in his honor. Today visitors may take guided lantern tours through New Cave. While walking along the primitive trails,

Big free-tailed bat.

they can still see wing and leg bones of these bats.

Pallid Bat and Western Pipistrelle

Pallid bats and western pipistrelles are common in the arid and semiarid lands of the Southwest, and both inhabit the rugged limestone canyons and gypsum flats of Carlsbad Caverns National Park. Both species have been taken at Longview Spring, Rattlesnake Spring, and Spider Cave Seep. Pallid bats also were captured at Grammer Spring and pipistrelles at the Potholes.

Western pipistrelles are very early fliers and can be observed flying well before the sun sets behind canyon walls. In contrast, pallid bats typically emerge from their roost after sunset. Rock crevices in cliffs are favorite daytime shelters of both species. A number of pipistrelles also have been found roosting beneath rocks and boulders lying on the ground. Pallid bats, and to a lesser degree pipistrelles, also use buildings. For many years a summer colony of pallid bats occupied the porch of the adobe pumphouse at Rattlesnake Spring. Both species occasionally roost in caves and mines. At the park, pipistrelles have been caught in Carlsbad Cavern and a pallid bat in the mouth of the large natural entrance.

During the summer pallid bats typically form small maternity colonies, the largest ones containing about 200 animals. Nursery colonies of pipistrelles may contain as many as 50 individuals, but some mothers and their infants also have been found roosting alone. Little information is available about the winter habits of these bats. Neither species is known to migrate, but pallid

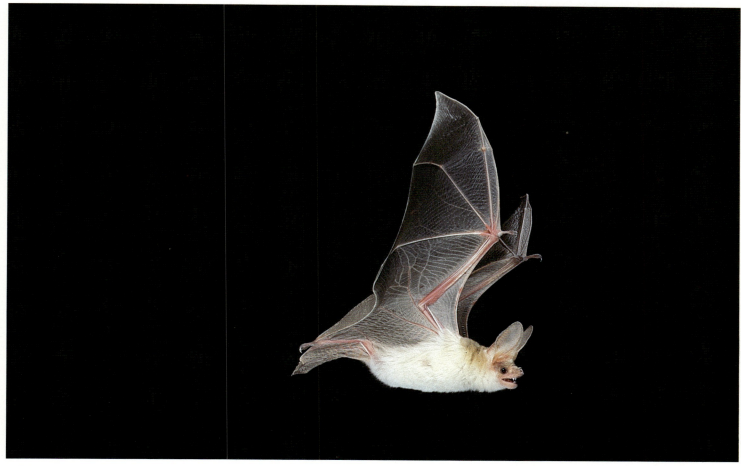

Pallid bat.

With wingspans of only nine inches, western pipistrelles are the smallest bats in the park. These early fliers are seen drinking over pools of water well before sunset.

bats may travel short distances between their winter and summer homes. Although no winter records of either species are known for New Mexico, both species surely hibernate in the state.

Hoary Bat and Red Bat

These foliage-roosting bats are among the most beautifully colored bats in the United States. The silver-tipped hairs of hoary bats produce a frosted appearance over most of their body, while red bats vary in color from an orange red to rusty red. In both cases, their coloration helps to conceal the animals when they hang among the leaves of trees and other vegetation. Red bats sometimes resemble dead leaves and even have been mistaken for certain kinds of fruits. The frosted hairs of hoary bats noticeably mimic leaves glistening in the sun. While roosting in these relatively exposed sites, these bats may partially cover themselves with their furred tail

membranes to help conserve body heat.

Both species are solitary bats, hanging singly or in family groups consisting of a mother and her young. At the park a red bat was found hanging among the leaves of a pear tree at Rattlesnake Spring. Although these species prefer to roost in trees, at one time or another they have been found in caves. In fact, the other seven records of red bats at the park are from animals found within caves — six in Carlsbad Cavern and one in Deep Cave. One animal was a pregnant female captured alive in the lunch room of

Red bats are migratory, but some populations also are known to hibernate on a regular basis.

Carlsbad Cavern during early summer. Wing bones of hoary bats also have been found in the cavern.

Hoary bats are highly migratory. Waves of migrants pass through New Mexico each spring, and during this period these bats may appear anywhere in the state. It was during spring migration that hoary bats were netted over Rattlesnake Spring and the earthen pond by the lagoons. Females apparently move through the state and head for more northerly locations to bear and raise their young, while males seek the cool montane forests of the state for the remainder of the summer. Evidence indicates that hoary bats head for wintering ground south of the United States during fall migration. Thus far, there are no records of hoary bats in the state during the winter nor is there any evidence that they hibernate anywhere on a regular basis.

Opposite page:
A hoary bat hangs among the leaves of a pinyon pine. The bat's thick fur provides insulation while roosting in these relatively exposed sites.

Red bats also are migratory, but unlike hoary bats, some populations also are known to hibernate regularly. In New Mexico, red bats usually are found associated with cottonwoods and other deciduous trees growing along watercourses in the southern part of the state. In contrast to hoary bats, red bats raise their young within the state's boundaries. Red bats have not been observed in New Mexico during the winter months and apparently migrate to other regions. Some populations of red bats migrate long distances to reach their winter destinations while others just hibernate locally. This species is known to winter in coastal California and southeastern United States, and some animals are known to hibernate in trees as far north as the Ohio River Valley.

A silver-haired bat is camouflaged while roosting on a dead tree trunk.

Silver-haired Bat

Silver-haired bats are known to migrate and hibernate, and it is during these periods that they show up at Carlsbad Caverns National Park. A male was captured at Rattlesnake Spring during spring migration, and two bats have been collected in Carlsbad Cavern — a female in winter and a male in spring. The seasonal distribution of silver-haired bats in New Mexico is similar to that of hoary bats in that females are absent during the summer while males, at least in June and July, inhabit montane forests. The winter-taken specimen from the cavern provides evidence of hibernation in the state.

During warmer months, various types of shelter provided by trees seem to be the favorite roosting sites for silver-haired bats. They roost behind pieces of loose bark, inside woodpecker holes and other tree cavities, in the open ends of fallen branches and tree trunks, and some have even been found in bird nests. Not surprisingly, they also have been found behind wooden shingles, in open sheds and other buildings, in piles of lumber and fence posts, and in other man-made shelters. Hibernating sites include hollow trees, spaces underneath bark, buildings, rock crevices, caves, and mines. Recently a female was found hibernating in a rodent burrow in Indiana. Silver-haired bats roost singly or in groups of less than 15. There are no reliable records of large aggregations of this species during any time of the year.

Although big brown bats are primarily woodland animals in New Mexico, they occur in desert habitats of the park.

Big Brown Bat

Big brown bats are primarily woodland animals in New Mexico. They are most abundant in forests of ponderosa pine but also inhabit the lower woodlands of pinyon and juniper and higher forests of spruce and fir. Big brown bats also occur in the arid and semiarid habitats of Carlsbad Caverns National Park. For example, a female was caught at Rattlesnake Spring in late May, and a few animals have been netted leaving Carlsbad Cavern through its small natural entrance. Lactating females also have been taken at Longview Spring in August.

During the summer, big brown bats form nursery colonies averaging about 100 animals; however, there are reports of colonies with as few as eight individuals and as many as 700. Rock crevices, hollow trees, and various types of buildings serve as maternity roosts for mothers and their young.

Big brown bats hibernate, and there is at least one winter specimen from New Mexico. In preparation for hibernation, they accumulate much excess body fat to be used as energy reserves during winter dormancy; at this time, up to one third of their body weight is fat. Winter roosts include caves, mines, and occasionally buildings. Some individuals may travel relatively short distances to reach these winter retreats, but long-distance travel under natural circumstances in this species is not known. Experiments have shown, however, that big brown bats are able to find their way home after being displaced hundreds of miles.

Townsend's Big-eared Bat

Townsend's big-eared bats are year-round residents of New Mexico. They occupy habitats ranging from lowland deserts up to mixed coniferous forests of spruce, fir, Douglas fir, and pine. This species is rather sedentary, making at most only short seasonal movements from summer foraging grounds to winter shelters.

In the winter these bats hibernate in caves and mine tunnels and roost singly or in clusters which may include both sexes. At these winter sites they often curl their long ears against their neck to help reduce heat loss. At Carlsbad

Townsend's big-eared bat.

Caverns National Park, individuals have been located at Carlsbad Cavern in November, Goat Cave in December, and Deep Cave in January.

During the warmer months, a male was netted over Longview Spring and a lactating female at the Potholes. Summer retreats of Townsend's big-eared bats include caves, abandoned mines, and buildings. Here females form nursery colonies that usually contain from a dozen to a couple of hundred individuals. During this period, males roost alone even when sharing shelters containing nursery colonies.

Myotis

Five species of myotis inhabit Carlsbad Caverns National Park, but only the fringed myotis, cave myotis, and California myotis are common residents. To date, skulls of Yuma myotis provide the only evidence of this species in the park, and the presence of long-legged myotis was recently established when a female was netted over Longview Spring in May. In addition to these five species, small-footed myotis are strongly suspected to occur in the park.

In New Mexico, long-legged myotis almost exclusively inhabit cool coniferous forests. Based on more than 700 specimens collected in the state, most have been captured in ponderosa pine communities or in forests at higher elevations; about a dozen came from grassland habitats. The Carlsbad specimen and the dozen from grassland areas most likely represent migrating individuals. During the summer long-legged myotis establish maternity colonies that often contain hundreds of bats. Nurseries have been found in tree cavities, under loose bark, in buildings, and

Ears curled against its neck to reduce heat loss, a Townsend's big-eared bat hibernates on the ceiling of a limestone cave.

The fringe of hair along the trailing edge of the tail membrane easily distinguishes the fringed myotis from the other four myotis which inhabit the park.

occasionally in rock crevices. There are a few records of this species hibernating in caves and mines, but for the most part the winter range of long-legged myotis and the distance to which they travel to wintering sites are unknown.

Fringed myotis in New Mexico inhabit a wide spectrum of habitats, from desert lowlands up to mixed coniferous forests. Within these habitats, favored maternity sites include caves, mines, and buildings. Two nursery colonies of fringed myotis have been located in the park. One is located in Left Hand Tunnel of Carlsbad Cavern, a section of cave lying 700 feet underneath the ground. Over the years females have formed colonies numbering no more than 100 individuals in various sections of this tunnel. The other nursery colony is located in Lake Cave and usually contains a few hundred individuals. Fringed myotis also have been captured at Longview Spring, Rattlesnake Spring,

and the Potholes. This species hibernates in caves, mines, and perhaps buildings, but the magnitude of their movements to these wintering sites after maternity colonies break up in late summer is unknown.

Cave myotis are common inhabitants of limestone caves and gypsum sinkholes of southeastern New Mexico. At Carlsbad Caverns National Park, males and pregnant females have been captured at Rattlesnake Spring and males at the earthen pond by the lagoons. The only other record at the park includes a group of males roosting with female fringed myotis on the ceiling of Left Hand Tunnel in Carlsbad Cavern. Cave myotis are much more common in the gypsum flats east of the park. During the summer females sometimes congregate in large colonies numbering in the thousands. Favorite roosting sites include caves, mines, and occasionally buildings. Cave myotis are known to travel short distances to their wintering quarters, but most probably hibernate in caves close to their summer homes.

California myotis and small-footed myotis are closely related species that have very similar habits and habitat preferences. In New Mexico both can be found living in desert and montane situations. At a number of arid localities in southwestern New Mexico, both species are commonly caught feeding and drinking over the same water holes. However, in the southeastern part of the state California myotis are much more common. At the park, California myotis have been netted at Longview Spring, Grammer Spring, Rattlesnake Spring, and Spider Cave Seep and found alive in Carlsbad Cavern. Small-footed myotis have not yet been captured in the park but are known to occur along the eastern escarpment of the Guadalupe Mountains outside the park. Although skulls from Carlsbad Cavern were once identified as this species, reexamination showed them to be remains of California and Yuma myotis. Both California and small-footed myotis are crevice-dwellers, roosting almost anywhere they can squeeze into. For example, roosts include spaces between cracks in rocks, under bark, behind boards, in holes of banks, and inside abandoned swallow nests. Although females and their young may roost alone, small colonies numbering in the twenties have been located for each species. For hibernation, these bats seek caves and mines, but the extent of travel to their winter retreats is unknown.

Skeletal remains of Yuma myotis provide the only evidence of this myotis in the park. Skulls were located in Carlsbad Cavern during the early 1950s. In New Mexico this species is much more common in the western and northern part of the state. Here Yuma myotis are locally common in woodlands growing along streams and other waterways of desert and grassland communities and in pinyon-juniper habitats where open water is nearby. Large maternity colonies of Yuma myotis, sometimes numbering in the thousands, have been reported in caves, mines, buildings, and bridges. The extent to which this species hibernates and migrates is unknown.

Yuma myotis are rare in the southeastern portion of New Mexico. To date, skulls found in Carlsbad Cavern provide the only evidence of this species in the park.

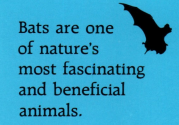

Bats are one of nature's most fascinating and beneficial animals.

A Need for Conservation

Unfortunately, the population of freetails at Carlsbad Cavern is not the only colony of bats that has experienced a major decline during recent decades. In fact, reports of declines in bat populations come from nearly every part of the world. Several species of bats already are extinct, and others are near extinction.

The major threat to the survival of bats is man. As shown earlier, man's use of agricultural pesticides can have detrimental effects on populations of insect-eating bats. Even minor disturbances of bats at their hibernating sites and maternity roosts may be fatal. For example, unnecessary arousal of hibernating bats due to the presence of people may result in the loss of too much stored fat. Depleted energy supplies may cause many bats to starve before their food supply reemerges in spring. Loss of habitat as a result of the constant need for more space for people, their crops, and livestock also is taking its toll on bats as well as many other animals.

In addition to the unintentional killing of bats, large numbers are deliberately killed and thousands of roosts are destroyed each year. Public health is the most common reason for this destruction, even though bats rarely transmit disease to humans. The removal of bats from the wild for scientific and educational purposes, as well as for food, also has been a contributing factor in declines of certain populations. The impact of all these factors is magnified because bats have low reproductive rates.

A number of conservation efforts have been designed specifically to reduce disturbances to roosting bats and to increase available roosting sites. Special gates are being installed in front of cave entrances which allow easy passage for bats but exclude people. Bat roosts are being restored as in the case of Bat Cave at the park. Bat houses and towers are being placed in forests and backyards to attract insect-eating bats. Besides these efforts, many countries also offer bats some legal protection. In the United States a number of species are protected under the federal Endangered Species Act. Bats have been protected at Carlsbad Caverns National Park since 1923.

Although these conservation efforts do provide some protection, they will never be totally effective without changing people's attitude toward bats. Negative attitudes must be replaced with an understanding of the ecological, economic, and scientific value of bats. This goal can be achieved through education.

Concern about the worldwide decline of bats has led to the formation of Bat Conservation International, an organization whose purpose is to preserve bat populations around the world and to improve public attitudes toward bats. Information about this organization, including membership and subscription to its newsletter, may be obtained by writing to:

Bat Conservation International
Post Office Box 162603
Austin, Texas 78716-2603
U.S.A.

The logo of Bat Conservation International is based on an ancient Chinese design. The circle of bats encloses a stylized tree – the Chinese symbol of life. Each bat signifies one of the five great happinesses of life: health, prosperity, long life, good luck, and tranquility.

Acknowledgments

Although most of our efforts in completing this book took place in the last few years, all three of us became involved with the bats at Carlsbad Caverns in the early 1970s. We suspect that thoughts of writing this book first entered our minds during those early years. Since then many park personnel have contributed to our efforts. Their cooperation, assistance, and friendship through the years are greatly appreciated. We especially thank Gary Ahlstrand, Katie Bridwell, Cliff Chetwin, Bobby Crisman, William Dunmire, Donna Giannantonio, Pat Kilgore, Margaret Littlejohn, Dave Machado, Dan Murphy, Maudie Nelson, Bob Peters, Charlie Peterson, Bennie Phillips, John Roth, Phil Van Cleave, and Bruce Weber. We also express our sincere gratitude to other friends, colleagues, and relatives who have aided us in numerous ways and who have led directly to the improvement and completion of this book. We especially thank Chris Altenbach, Lyle Berger, Troy Best, Ann Bonda, Tony Burgess, Denny Constantine, Jay Druecker, Don Duszynski, Patty Gegick, Greg Geluso, Marianne Geluso, Keith Geluso, Barbara Hayhome, Robert Hollander, Damon Kerbo, Diannia Kerbo, Rick Manning, Gary McCracken, and Dave Sutherland. We also appreciate the cooperation and assistance of Terry Yates (Museum of Southwestern Biology), Don Wilson (National Museum of Natural History), and Trish Freeman (University of Nebraska State Museum) for providing access to specimens and museum facilities under their direction. We thank the Cave Research Foundation for use of their field station at Carlsbad Caverns and the biology departments at UNO and UNM for providing funds for the many trips to and from the park. We wish to dedicate this book to our parents and families for years of patience and support during our studies of bats and caves.

Black and White Photographs courtesy of the National Park Service
Color Photographs by J. Scott Altenbach and Ronal C. Kerbo: JSA pages 2-8, 12 (bats), 13, 15, 16, 19, 23-29, front cover, and back cover; RCK pages 1, 9-11, 12 (spring), 17-18, and front cover (inset)
Drawing of Bat Cave by Beth Dennis
Maps by Pam Lungé
Distribution map after Hall (1981) The Mammals of North America
Edited by Rose Houk
Designed by Christina Watkins
Reviewed by James Findley
Coordinated by Robert Peters
Printed by Lorraine Press, Inc., Salt Lake City, Utah

APPENDIX 1.— Bats Inhabiting Carlsbad Caverns National Park

Common Name	Scientific Name
(FAMILY)	(FAMILY)
(Species)	(Species)
FREE-TAILED BATS	MOLOSSIDAE
Big Free-tailed Bat	*Tadarida macrotis*
Constantine's Free-tailed Bat*	*Tadarida constantinei**
Mexican Free-tailed Bat	*Tadarida brasiliensis mexicana*
Pocketed Free-tailed Bat	*Tadarida femorosacca*
COMMON BATS	VESPERTILIONIDAE
Big Brown Bat	*Eptesicus fuscus*
California Myotis	*Myotis californicus*
Cave Myotis	*Myotis velifer*
Fringed Myotis	*Myotis thysanodes*
Hoary Bat	*Lasiurus cinereus*
Long-legged Myotis	*Myotis volans*
Pallid Bat	*Antrozous pallidus*
Red Bat	*Lasiurus borealis*
Silver-haired Bat	*Lasionycteris noctivagans*
Townsend's Big-eared Bat	*Plecotus townsendii*
Western Pipistrelle	*Pipistrellus hesperus*
Yuma Myotis	*Myotis yumanensis*

*extinct

APPENDIX 2— Wingspan and Forearm Length of Bats Inhabiting Carlsbad Caverns National Park

Common Name	Wingspan*		Forearm Length**	
	millimeters	inches	millimeters	inches
Big Free-tailed Bat	427	16.8	58.3 – 61.4	2.3 – 2.4
Hoary Bat	397	15.6	52.0 – 55.0	2.0 – 2.2
Pallid Bat	363	14.3	49.8 – 55.1	2.0 – 2.2
Pocketed Free-tailed Bat	345	13.6	44.7 – 46.7	1.7 – 1.8
Big Brown Bat	332	13.1	44.5 – 50.0	1.7 – 2.0
Mexican Free-tailed Bat	300	11.8	40.2 – 44.5	1.6 – 1.8
Red Bat	300	11.8	38.5 – 42.3	1.5 – 1.7
Cave Myotis	296	11.7	42.1 – 45.9	1.7 – 1.8
Townsend's Big-eared Bat	293	11.5	39.3 – 45.3	1.5 – 1.8
Fringed Myotis	289	11.4	40.5 – 44.6	1.6 – 1.8
Silver-haired Bat	289	11.4	38.3 – 42.4	1.5 – 1.7
Long-legged Myotis	264	10.4	37.0 – 41.1	1.5 – 1.6
Yuma Myotis	235	9.3	31.7 – 34.9	1.2 – 1.4
California Myotis	230	9.1	30.8 – 34.1	1.2 – 1.3
Western Pipistrelle	227	8.9	30.8 – 33.7	1.2 – 1.3

*average value; data from a variety of sources.
**minimum-maximum values; measurements based on New Mexican specimens.